RED CLAY SUITE

CRAB ORCHARD SERIES IN POETRY

Open Competition Award

RED CLAY SUITE

HONORÉE FANONNE JEFFERS

Crab Orchard Review

&

Southern Illinois University Press

Carbondale

21 20 19 18   6 5 4 3

The Crab Orchard Series in Poetry is a joint publishing venture of
Southern Illinois University Press and *Crab Orchard Review*. This
series has been made possible by the generous support of the Office
of the President of Southern Illinois University and the Office of
the Vice Chancellor for Academic Affairs and Provost at Southern
Illinois University Carbondale.

Crab Orchard Series in Poetry Editor: Jon Tribble
Open Competition Award Judge for 2006: Dorianne Laux

Library of Congress Cataloging-in-Publication Data

Jeffers, Honorée Fanonne, date.
  Red clay suite / Honorée Fanonne Jeffers.
      p. cm. — (Crab Orchard series in poetry)
   ISBN-13: 978-0-8093-2760-7 (pbk. : alk. paper)
   ISBN-10: 0-8093-2760-0 (pbk. : alk. paper)
   I. Title.

PS3560.e365R43 2007
813'.6 — dc22

                                                  2006026252

Printed on recycled paper. ♻

The paper used in this publication meets the minimum
requirements of American National Standard for Information
Sciences—Permanence of Paper for Printed Library Materials,
ANSI Z39.48-1992.∞

For Mama, for home

Tall trees catch wind.

—GRANDPA CHARLIE

Contents

Acknowledgments

Grateful acknowledgment goes to the following journals that first published these poems (some in earlier form with different names)

American Poetry Review—"Cotton Field Sestina"
Callaloo—"Blues Aubade (or, Revision of the Lean, Post-Modernist Pastorale)" "Eatonton One," "The Blues I Don't Want to Remember," "Here, One of Your Four Women," and "The Little Boy Who Will Be My Father"
Crab Orchard Review—part 2 of "Reunion Scripture"
5AM—"Their Splendid" and "The Subject of Gardening"
The Gettysburg Review—"Red Clay Suite"
Gulf Coast—"I've Been Up Late Reading the Book of Poems You Inscribed and Mailed to Me"
The Iowa Review—"Suddenly in Grace"
Meridians: Feminism, Race, Transnationalism—"Hawk Hoof Tea," "Upon Learning That my Indian Student Is a Sundancer," "dirty south moon," "Driving Interstate West through Georgia," and "Oklahoma Naming"
Obsidian III: Black Literature in Review—"The Two Marys," which appears here under the title "Another Easter Poem"
PMS: PoetryMemoirStory—part 1 of "Reunion Scripture" and "What Is Written for Me"
Saranac Review—"Lexicon"

Gratitude first and always to the Creator, from Whom all words and life descend, and to the ancestors for watching over, especially Charlie and Alvester James. Rest in peace and goodness.

To my family: Trellie James Jeffers, Valjeanne Jeffers-Thompson, Sidonie Jeffers, Toussaint Thompson, Mikail Thompson, and especially my niece, my baby sister, Gabrielle Thompson.

To my red clay folk: Vera James and Mrs. Annie Pearl James.

To Lucille Clifton, Hank Lazer, Jerry Ward Jr., Maggie Anderson, Ed Ochester, Elizabeth Alexander, Marilyn Nelson, David Lynn, Circe Sturm, Robert Warrior, Geary Hobson, Charles Henry Rowell, Rodney Jones, Allison Joseph, and Jon Tribble.

To Natasha Trethewey, John Alexander Frazier, and Dolen Perkins-Valdez, patient listeners; Remica Bingham and James William Richardson Jr., peerless, loving critics; Cherise Pollard, sassy, kind, and brilliant; Kimberly Clark-Waddy, before time, boyfriends, and fashion sense; Andrea Franckowiak, my Rock; Rekha Subramanian, darling, strong Goddess; Tony Medina, radical touchstone; Carlos Wise, God's child; and Herman Beavers, a brother-friend for this life and all the ones after.

To those poets who took that river walk with me in Esopus, New York, back in the summer of 1996: faith continues.

To Afaa Michael Weaver, poet, elder, and teacher, who urged me to claim courage and testify: your love and guidance will never be forgotten.

To Dorianne Laux, thank you, thank you so much for seeing.

PROLOGUE

Red Clay Suite

I was five when I journeyed to the land of red clay,
that place of my grandmother—she was destroyed by red clay.

An old wives' tale: a big-bellied woman should eat dirt.
And who wouldn't want to birth babies who crave red clay?

My own mama was born in an abandoned slave shack.
She never forgot the hot prison of her red clay.

Meriney: the color of sun's heat, overripe peaches,
most of my cousins, clotted blood, lovely red clay.

I'm called *Big Country* for my southern wails, the tune
down in my gut, my drama for one sight of red clay.

Blues, the cotton field like a mind stripped clean
of memory: these are the people's stories, their epic red clay.

Why my father hated me and wished my death, I don't know,
but maybe Daddy saved me, digging my grave in red clay.

Can I get a witness is this preacher's plea, needful moan—
that great getting up day, Jesus will come home to red clay.

1 MIGRATION CANTOS

Word on Earth

I take the land as text, as a preacher might,
or a deceived ecstatic hoping for signs.
Now prairie, where I've squatted
for three years but before,
I found my mind in red clay.

Come back, child is a call too strong
for me, a woman grown—June, the month
of emancipation, decides the time.
I'm headed home out of Oklahoma,
on to Georgia.

I follow the interstate line, straight
like a good girl, then down.
Never as the crow flies, but through back
roads my folk wouldn't trust fifty years ago.
I seek those blues-tinged drawls, clingstone
peaches, clichéd porch swings,
keep on past cattle, flat fields, oil wells.

Sixteen hours of driving in tornado
season, my anxiously searching
for telltale gray-green horizons
in the rearview mirror.
Once leaving Georgia and reaching
an unknown part of Illinois—
I can't say where now—
I saw a funnel cloud.
The sky was lovely, an unholy shade.
Then a shitting down of hail:
the Word written on earth.

I knew the end was upon me.
My bowels almost released—
I felt like Janie.
I prayed with a clean heart
then drove through to clear skies.
I swore to myself, to my mama,
to God above,
I'd never leave Dixie if I saw it again.
I lied, forgive me.
Red clay, I lied.

Passing

*Because of the enduring stability of the Cherokee clan system there
was no such thing as a "half-breed," even in the late 18th century.
Matrilineal kinship provided the blood substance of identity, and a
child's identity was determined solely by the mother, whether she
be Cherokee or of another tribe . . .*

—CIRCE STURM

What would I be if she were still alive?
If that great, great, great Cherokee woman
had walked the Trail, signed
the tribal roll instead of committing

the sin of loving a slave,
atsi nahsa'i?
If she had refused his children?
If she had married the right man,

a free Cherokee and not a slave?
If she'd remembered the old ways
I'd be full—of language, community, blood.
I'd be driving through my home—

this Oklahoma which is ugly as I pass it by—
instead of headed to Georgia
where my black family lives.
I'd feel safe when I spotted my tribal

sign as I sped down the highway,
Entering Cherokee Nation.
I wouldn't remember I'm a mixed-blood,
a mistake, a buffalo hair.

That she's lost to history—
the copper woman,
half-breed Henry's mama.
That she escaped the Trail,

somehow,
though no one in our family
knows the details.
That her people,

the Cherokees, were removed
from Georgia, forced out West to clear
the way for inland cotton.
That when they left

they took their slaves along, didn't free them,
and with the diseases, rapes, killings,
blotted memories,
the journey where they cried,

when they got to Oklahoma the Cherokees
worked their slaves body and mind—
there's a reason
I hate the prairie so.

That I don't know her real name,
only that she was called Amanda, Mandy,
something like that,
and she had a black husband

whom I hoped she loved,
but I know for sure she had lots of children
and those children had children
(and so on and so forth)

and we are the crossroads.
I have no proof that I'm a real Cherokee,
so maybe I need to forget
a woman who lied or hid or got lost

or fought
so she could keep her name off that roll.
What would have happened if she hadn't stayed?
If a woman hadn't made a home

with her dark family on Georgia clay,
entered strangeness and limbo?
Within, without—but alive?
I keep driving, *Leaving Cherokee Nation.*

Giving Thanks for Water

Before moving to Oklahoma,
I read up on the Tulsa riots,
was shocked—I thought they only
did things like that back
home in the Deep South.
I guess I was wrong.

Ugliness is an obsession of mine—
I read the news on 1921
as if that year wasn't gone,
disappeared in smoke,
those judges waiting
for the last witnesses, stubborn old folk,
to die and take their goddamned
memories into grace:

Dick and Sarah black shoeshine man
white elevator woman I heard
tell he grabbed her did he grab
her white grabbed her woman Molotov
cocktails dropped black burned
to Sodom's ash man dozens bodies
stacked up hundreds unmarked
graves thousands I heard tell

Skirting this city's edge,
I see a few trees in shy clumps.
I'm driving past Tulsa,
taking a roundabout way home,
with knowledge vindicating—
a bit—my sweet Georgia.
This morning, I took a shower
and gave thanks for water,
for the cleanliness next to God.

If you please Little
Africa burning one girl hid
in a pigpen please she lived
through Black Wall Street
burning if you please

Thank You, Maker,
for swine, filth, and Noah's rain.
Thank you, Lord,
for memory's long-lived,
pointing finger.

An Angel, Unaware

Mrs. Williams' face was pleading when she spoke of her god to me.
　　　　—LANCE JEFFERS

As the plane rose, I broached faith
first. I know that's not popular,
even dangerous these days, but my seatmate

was convicted, mentioning *The Muslims*,
how *crazy* they were, *their ingratitude*
over our invasion. I suspected

where the talk would lead—
he was an accountant, though sweet.
I remembered my Bible—

I should be generous, lest I entertain
an angel, unaware. I nodded but declared,
Every human has a right to stay alive.

I thought of my father, his slaps,
his belief that we should love
his cruelty, and I started really

liking this bigot next to me,
dutiful daughter that I remain.
I tried to convince my seatmate,

*You know, we're going to stand
one day in front of our Maker.*
He looked confused, praised the President

despite Katrina,
that disaster with one name,
No one to blame there.

I sang the colored blues: New Orleans,
black folk alive, frying in the Superdome,
or dead and bloated in Lake Pontchartrain.

Rats and such,
but he came back to the war,
fallen soldiers, necessary sacrifices.

I thought of my father again,
how I waited for the good
to come out of that man.

I wonder—more than I should—if Daddy
was saved in those last days
when he started hedging his bets,

got a healthy taste for the Bible,
and took to praying.

The Compass of Moss

Winter, I arrived for a residency
in a tiny, white Ohio college town.
Once it was Underground Railroad country.
People there hid runaways following
the North Star trail to freedom.
That might be,
but I was scared in that fairytale village.
Don't most stories hold a Grimm twist,
a flaxen-locked dame ravished by dark beast—
why not the same in reverse?

At night I tried to shake the past.
John Brown's body lay moldering,
Harriet Tubman's as well.
I was among friends, but what
of their whiteness, my dark skin?
I roamed my rooms, dressed for disaster,
shoes by my bed's edge.
This was hell.

Then daylight and I was fine,
walked the Middle Path—
sure a fly in buttermilk, but *all right*—
stopped to check oaks (for Harriet)
to see if that slave tale held true,
that moss grew only on the north side.

For once I got it: when the clouds
cloaked the guiding Star,
the compass of moss pointed the way
for poor souls. Follow.
Then I teared up, spilled over,
wiped my face. Shaken.
Why couldn't I let it go?

Write one poem on moss
and its odd history, then disconnect.
I sipped my coffee.
Above, a murder of crows
moved together, called down to me,
Ah ha, ah ha, so now you think you're free?

Let Blood Go

East, then south, the land is prettier,
though rough, wild. Brightness peeking
between trees, a pair of coy eyes.
Arkansas, Tennessee, finally Mississippi.
Some home feeling inside—
Negro territory.
There's no cotton, nappy, overgrown,
by this long highway, but new grass,
and trees, branches twisted:
a back broken down the spine.

Should I feel afraid driving here
when I know this dystopia,
can name the sins of familiars?
There's comfort in Confederate
flags, gun racks in backs of pickups,
coldness in the eyes of some whites,
resignation in the eyes of others.
Black folk rolling, surviving—
some angry, but most let blood go.

Nostalgia washes over me.
When I stop to eat in Holly Springs,
I order fried chicken, look the young
waitress right in her (of course) blue eyes,
wish I was a brother committing a crime,
reckless eyeballing,
maybe whistling for Emmett Till,
but this child wants to please—*Yes, ma'am*.
Born about sixteen years ago
with a guiltless, bare soul.

And I am a woman,
same as what this child—
blue eyes—standing before me will become,
a woman like Emmett's mother.
Blues eyes, this land—O Mamie, Mama, Mississippi
bless this blood searching east and south,
and your son's heart buried,
then unearthed from kin dirt.

Cotton Field Sestina

The bolls by the side of the road—
at first this picture of startling cream lies
to the senses—maybe snow?—but the blues
rises up, the heat rises up, the sweat—so much water
down my neck. At last I see the dusty
flecks are cotton, what I should know in my gut.

On the radio, the song plucked on a gut
string reminds me this is a hard road
I tried to leave behind haloed by dust,
along with the poetics of lies.
I think of ancestry: copper folk gone, salt water
Africans bent over the land, original blues.

Come back home, girl. Isn't my blues
about reconciliation, not escape? What my gut
hollers, thus speaks the guilty water
chattering down my face? This road
is my lonely path cut through trees, lying
like a frog-fed snake in the dust.

I remember: feet caked with red dust,
tongues coated with loud blues.
I remember: old men telling them lies
and their good deep laughter in the gut—
what waits for me down this road
if I could cross the big water

of my fear, of my guilt, drink the water
thirsty in the women's veins, shake the dust
from my clothes and whisper the road,
hear the country voices raised in drylongso blues.
First, I have to crawl through my mother's gut
past the long braid of her lies.

My mother, my mama, she calls me a liar,
she denies me her waters,
turns me out of her sweet gut
if I don't shake loose my fist of grave dust,
if I don't stop writing down my blues,
if I don't trot behind her on her smooth road.

Come back home, girl to what lies in Georgia dust:
no love in truth's water, no birdsong blues,
no home in my gut—cotton by the roadside.

Eatonton (Two)

I sit on the porch of a small, gray house
in the town where Harris met
and stole Remus, Rabbit,
the stories of those who call this place home.
An agrarian lack now in this yard:

no flowers rioting around windows,
or that one pine tree my first love
and I leaned against when we kissed.
My grandmother dead six years—that lost
Eatonton appears only on my page.

The tomatoes, squash, collard greens
in the furrowed garden gone, too,
from the backyard where I played, sharecroppers'
progeny, assured of place,
safe inside the walls of a segregated street

over the tracks,
calmed by what I could name.
At least, something I claimed.
Sitting on this porch,
I see the pale children of Harris

walk to the corner,
unheeding history,
mingling with darker brethren.
White kids don't sneak these days.
They stand unafraid in this bad, black

neighborhood, bob heads to music of cars
passing, hand over money, in glaring
daylight, for joints rolled tight into fists.
Some things don't change.
The street remains segregated—

not even poor whites would live here—
and there is the scent of honeysuckle
from blocks over. The old tropes:
a woman, grown and moved away,
returns once a year

to sit on a porch, faithful stage,
feel guilty about leaving back in the day,
and wait for her first love
who pressed her into a pine tree
cut down years ago.

That love, a man who stays outdoors long
into night, unheeding
the waiting woman who left as a girl,
tries to coax a broke-down car into life.
And brothers on the corner, perennials,

talking trash, Rabbit's kin
chasing what they can't catch
in this stolen, red scrap of home,
this bottom, what Harris snatched
without a blush—the briar patch.

Driving Interstate West through Georgia

Already I am an outsider, a visitor
seldom and hasty to my community
of pecan, cedar, pine, oak. A forgetful witness
to the smell of peaches liquoring the air.

I see this land the way I remember
and do the same for childhood love—
the rough hand that touched me
but didn't scrape down to bone.

Like those Africans choking down
mouthfuls of home before they were loaded
onto the boats, this place
might be gone from me soon.

The clucking of grown folks'
voices as they prayed over daily meat,
the branch cradling the blood's neck,
patch of green fed by offhand screams.

If this earth is denied me, then what do I know?
That before you travel to the prairie's fields,
you must follow the southern tangle?
That if you try to pull up something

unfinished from the ground, the clotted
sounds of lament will cling to the roots?

2 DARK PASTORAL

Blues Aubade
(or, Revision of the Lean, Post-Modernist Pastorale)

I'm going to work in the holy name of Cézanne
somewhere in here, but first, let's say

I take a walk with my spade to safe, blank territory,
and then surely I'll dig to distraction in spongy loam,

then see petals spread, a chorus round a lazy eye,
then reach an epiphany—the importance of memory—

which necessitates a recollection of a lover
lying on a bed sheet,

his sparrow-boned hand gesturing vaguely toward me.
At this point there is early light filtering through a glass

of wine so clean, almost white on the bedside table.
Then I'll find a reason to conjure Cézanne—

Cézanne! Cézanne! Cézanne!—
as my excuse to discuss the poems he painted on canvas.

Before I start meditating on the apple's green buttock,
I hope there is time for a second walk

to another field that breaks me down, for prayer
and work, the precarious undoing of my birth.

Boss man calling me out of my name, hoe
over my shoulder to attack the hard crust.

Some cotton, some peaches, weighty heat of this harvest—
I remember my baby when we parted this morning.

We loved, we cried, O never enough!
We squeezed the scuppernong into spirit, drank it down gladly.

Brother Bearden had a relief for this kind of life,
a collage of agrarian truths. In this picture,

see the woman carved into the foreground of sweat?
And there—over *there*—way in the corner?

Now, that's a rooster crowing up a revolution.

Mister Buzzard and Brother Crow

Nigger, your breed ain't metaphysical.
—ROBERT PENN WARREN

Cracker, your breed ain't exegetical.
—STERLING A. BROWN

Buzzard and Crow, philosophizing birds,
creatures pondering the passage of time.
Not of a feather, they fly to the place,
a rioted clearing once bright and fine.

Practical Crow pecks bugs in the dirt
while Buzzard looks round for dead meat,
finds none, lifts to a famous oak tree branch—
from his high seat, looks down at Crow below.

Long ago, Buzzard intones a lovely bass.
This land was crowded with flowers, bees.
I won't call it Eden—that's so cliché—
but don't you agree we've seen sweeter days?

The Crow cries out, impatient for *new* news.
Mr. Buzzard, I can see same's you.
Wheels in ruts, weevils in cotton, smoke stacks,
nightmares right in front of me.

This ain't never been no easy landscape.
Now what? I count on you for prophecy.
Buzzard clears his throat, intoning some more,
Well then, look past to see what's in front.

Can't you spell the mystery?
If I made it plain the fun would be lost,
but I'm plenty sure I gave you a good head start.
Says Crow, pecking in the dirt,

I don't follow your hints.
You know y'all is too deep for me
cause I just tend my perch and sing loud in church.
My life boils down to simple blues.

I don't question God or the devil—
I'm blind to your clues.
Buzzard shakes a bit on that oak tree branch.
He's determined not to lose advantage.

You don't fool me, you Crow thing, you.
I know your kind believes in hoodoo.
Crow feels a gap approaching fast.
Hoodoo, signs in the clouds,

proof of what's unseen:
I remember you saying that won't
for me, but behind your back
I do read. In the beginning, indeed—

Amen, hallelujah and all of that!
Let's go back to your clichés:
what about them two in the Garden,
what happened with that first fruit tree?

Ciphers, portents, Mr. Buzzard, come on!
Learn to spell your own prophecies.
Buzzard knows the discussion has ended.
Ahem—it appears I've been too quick.

And Crow, his black feathers slick and shining,
tries to hide his prideful sin.
*Thanks so much, but I'll withhold my judgment,
Mr. Buzzard, if you'll grant me leave.*

Buzzard tips his head, southern gentleman.
Please, I'm trying. Shall we meet Sunday next?
Crow replies as he takes flight—it's night
and he needs to get in the wind, *Mayhap, till then.*

The two birds part, not real comrades, nor sad,
hardened enemies, just birds, that's all.
I leave you with Buzzard who bows again,
and Brother Crow gives a last, laughing call.

Consider My Brother as the Rabbit

after Sterling A. Brown

Consider my brother as the Rabbit—
Bruh, not *Br'er*, as Mister Harris mangled
on the page. *Bruh*, like the sound of the hoe's
swing hitting the earth's face: *Take these blues—huh—*
*plant them in the garden—huh—*he's trying,
failing, to feed his Mrs. and them six
critters so imagine his bellyache
schemes, the fur slick as grease, the bow-legged
running from the night riders through the Big
House yard back to his paradise. Sweet, cramped
trickery of briars. All God's creatures'
mouths watering for a meal of his flesh.
At least get the name right; give him his due.
Take these blues—huh—plant them in the garden

dirty south moon

the moon is here   the moon
don't believe the sun arriving for its own sake
thrall of nostalgia beating

out *out* spot of moon   don't believe the sun
or the tattoo of beauty   childhood tableaux
thrall of nostalgia beating   white dress on clothesline

beauty's tattoo   childhood tableaux   meaning of dirt
clapboard church   white dress on clothesline
swaying in obligatory side to side

don't believe in dirt   clapboard church   believe a southern moon
believe in this   swaying from side to side
necklace of woman's body

southern moon   toomer's tune   truth of billie's tree
believe the necklace of a woman's body   that heavens
should be raining still

that billie's tree sings truth   a phrase draped
at wood's throat   heavens raining still
knife opening her from side to side

phrase draped at the wood's throat   a falling child starts
stops   crying   knife unlocking its mother
no staring at her face   her name is mary

child falling out   who stops crying   stomped upon
by men swelled pale with lies   no blink of its eyes
no staring at mother's face   no bewilderment at first light   who

child   nothing holy said   no prayers over dead trees
no new creatures flying   bewildered at first light   who
only old blues

nothing holy   you can't hear nobody pray   brother
your sister hung here   hangs   sister   you know old blues
night till morning   don't you refuse her   don't commit old sins

when that is your sister hanging there   she is
twisting   dying for ham's supposed sins
think of songs on dancing tongues

twisting
have you not begged God   a familiar   have you not sent
words dancing   sung songs spontaneous   then forgot

that sister's hands begging fire   for your own salvation
not for songs unheard or used   look
the moon   look   *look here*

Here, One of Your Four Women

for Nina Simone

Given a row to hoe, strain
until it yields justification.
A body drifting toward the grave;
or a girl too young to take her truth bravely;

or a lady grown, holding onto the men
who don't want her;
or the last of the line, broken—*Peaches*—
dueling the air with her fist.

Each with the hoe grasped, every
so often her fingers brandished
as weapon, pulling the scolding
weeds, unrepentant, from the ground.

Each dropping the hoe, salute making
her brow a space of shade.
Heat shimmying, same row,
wisdom (*shoot*—work on some more),

chords of light sneaking away.
Wait—is that a note of praise
pinched now from a scarlet-breasted
creature, lifting over the crown of trees?

Here, one of your four women, Nina.
What marks her mocked, mocking horizon?
Stilled, she sighs over a small,
freed something.

Quickened, that woman bends, rises, bends:
another row.

One Morning Soon

for Gwendolyn Brooks

I am you, rising,
blinking a poem while the light makes
a Sunday best place of clay.
Why am I not cheap or driven this day
like the others, don't have to shimmy
just to earn a penny or two
because that's what mammies do?
Is it because today I am you,
allowed to be at the front of the race?—
I'm approaching blasphemy.
Now for penance I'll climb on top of the testimony
rock appearing from nowhere.
That's supposed to be my space.
Roll my neck, flex my blackness,
hope that sassy stays in style
(ah blues, *blues*).

I'm wooing readers at their first sign of waking,
speaking verses (terza rima, I think).
Then through the window a pinprick of goodness
I can name and I decide to shimmy
just because I want to
not because that is what I (or my folk) do.
And because I've ceased my blasphemy,
I can lift on my words to your blessed poet's state,
and I am doubtless lovely.
I am you: Afro an aureole,
my wings two thick bouquets of collards.
I forget my fears of darkness.
I was headed upward all along:
Miss Lady, you would know.

Poem for Birds

I know why the caged bird sings . . .
PAUL LAWRENCE DUNBAR

I know why. I am closer than fire,
piled up sticks or gas leaking
from a stove, Sylvia or Anne roaming
the night drinking the sap of cloves.
If the wind blows left
and I outrun you, I'll kiss every
hair on my child's head.
I'll sing some unnamed tune.

Everything is pleasing if I choose
sick or tired, not both.
Eat my insides or lick the plate clean,
but I can't squeak a whistle
and snap my fingers.
Then my memory is lost—
this woman is a fragile thing:
She don't mean no harm, if you please.
Her mind's just wasting away.
I know, though I try not to say it.

Suffer the children to come to Jesus,
suffer the little girls to turn into wives,
suffer the little boys hearing mother
scream at breaking light,
suffer this weird sister's midnight plight
or suffer that man to keep his own counsel—
please don't look at your own sorry life.

I know why—
you should, too:
I am gun or knife of Margaret become Sethe
counting down two minutes to spare.
Now I spy a white hat sitting
tall in the sun's glare.
So I kiss each hair growing on that small head,
and kiss a set of cupid bow lips.
A navel string,
a bared throat.

Another Easter Poem

Mary had a baby . . .
What did she name him?
   —TRADITIONAL SPIRITUAL

Too late for me now
in this thirty-fifth year.
Maybe my body would obey,
but my fears of a child, my weakness,
would come roosting again.
I can't be that sky-sent woman alone
in her task, a pair of hands sewing
my son's death robe. A mother,
chained as saint, shouting out
loud the disorder of faith.
Knees wide open, no freedom
from the Spirit's battering ram.

Now my belly is rounded out with disuse.
What you gone name
Now my hands cup under this dusty womb.
What you gone name
Not even death curled up in here,
but salt spilling, phantom,
and my dream's neck snapped.
What you gone name

How could I justify the third morning,
my own blood's blood as wine?
How could I roll back the stone
to dam a goddamned grief?
What you gone name that pretty little baby?
Maybe I would have called him
man, prayer, bread.

I've Been Up Late Reading the Book of Poems
You Inscribed and Mailed to Me

And first thinking of my prairie father,
poet, and then of my red clay mother,
muse, and what she thought he might be one day,
what kind of man if his poems were made flesh.
And then thinking of your gift, how you speak
stillness or playfulness or rage. Your poems
are so wise, so why can't you be? The poems—

is this why she forgave the cruelty,
and then again loved a baritone voice,
why I'm reading your mind too late at night?
I hope confusion is not a true art.
Your poems are so kind, now why can't you be?
Mama wished the same from her own closed man's
blues, his Nebraska sun, her Georgia moon.

Their Splendid

I love your laughter arrogant and bold.
You are too splendid for this city street.
    —HELENE JOHNSON

I bet you try to think about
moonlight, just a spot of it,
instead of shouting—unashamed—
in the middle of the street.
O black man (yes *black*,
though pale notes relieved),
I wish (to God)
I could take back those Bad Scenes,
your hard grace,
my self-conscious suffering.
I want you to remember
a good thing but there wasn't much of that.
So I ask if you do think of me, first
consider something else:
Billie cloaked by Prez's tune
their last day together,
how he chided her
as usual, bravado's shadow.
His riff way too long, tinny and brave,
but she moved with him
as he played, her face glassed over
with music or her mad tragedy.
It didn't matter by then.
Her deeds, their deeds,
were done or were not.
                    Alright, what do I mean?
I mean, our own short story
shames me sometimes—
there was no real moonlight I can recall—

but if you think of me at all,
think of the bruises on an arm,
or a song's dying bleats.
What the voice, what the horn
wanted to say to each other but couldn't.
How the man, how the woman
both walked away that day.
That was it, really it.
And they left behind
their splendid, wounded noise.

The Blues I Don't Want to Remember

When I ended up locked
in a room between them.
My mother was sitting on the bed
twisting her hands while he beat

on the door demanding to be let in.
I was six and the song
of a man still could fool me.

Let Daddy in, sweetheart
Let your daddy in
I searched for this honey in anyone's
mouth for close to thirty years,

then I wised up—have I finally wised up?
Let Daddy in, baby
Come on, let your daddy in

I almost turned the knob that day
until my mother called to me:
Don't open that door
Child, don't open that door

Now I hear her threatening
as my pen scratches across this page.
She wants to remind me

that truth telling can leap on you
with backhanded fierceness,
leave a black and blue mark in the morning
that will throb through the night long.

What Is Written for Me

One man.
Screamed at me one night, liquor
lighting him up inside like a prophet.
I was a woman.
A *woman*,
but I followed him into that dark field,
anyway, unafraid as only
a child should be.
When I finally was sure he meant
to kill me—that's when my love
for him came down in a revelation.

Another man.
Slapped me with the open palm
of one hand, twisted my hair
around the fingers of the other.
He let go and I followed him.
I ascended a flight of stairs
and what awaited me there
in that upper room was a page torn
from the Book of Job:
Naked I came out of my mother's womb
and naked shall I return.

Any other man.
Sings sweetly to me,
Baby, I'm not your daddy.
A futile croon.
He'll be gone soon.
I don't want his singing
or his kindness.

I want my father, his ugly touches
that required, the confusion of blood.
I want someone who sired a girl
who should have stayed unborn,
this shameful woman child,
an easy prophecy.

Lexicon

for my mother

This is the end for you two, though he doesn't see
it or that he'll be dead in four years,
heart just stopping, but not this day

when he sits in the armchair
which sags under his will, reads a book.
You speak a simple word to him—

we are leaving for good this time—
but I lose what it is,
so quick to be gone.

Something to indicate that we won't be coming back,
no last chances
like his assuming he can show up at the shelter

or drive further down south
to Grandma's house to collect us.
Or, I get the moment wrong and he goes down

to the basement first, puts on a record
—Rachmaninoff, loud—
walks upstairs, and then he sits down,

opens up his book, ignores you,
stops, cocks his head in the fine, sensitive
way that I continue to adore, ignores you some more,

tries to find blues in that European music.
A paradox,
but that is my father, kind to strangers,

slapping one of us upside our heads
at home, searching for beauty
in everything except his family

or his own reflection,
not bothering to plead with you
like he has the other times,

I'm sorry, baby.
Don't go. Please don't go.
The way a man is supposed to in the best songs.

I want you to toss something hard at him.
I'm scared we will return.
I'm scared we won't return.

I'm so angry with you and I haven't yet learned
how much weaker than a girl a woman can be.
How silly I am to assume you are stronger than he.

How arrogant I am to assume you are not.
The point is that I live, you live,
whether my father's music plays or doesn't play,

and we are driving off in the truck,
Mama,
leaving him turning the pages of his book.

What is that word? Forget about it.
We leave him there.
We left.

3 RED CLAY REPRISE

The Little Boy Who Will Be My Father

for Robert Hayden and Sharon Olds

Rides on a train through the once frontier
because his mother finally has sent for him,
her remembered duty.

He has a tag around his wrist,
that's how he knows who he is.

I like to think of him this way:
skin of pale gold,
hair brushed into obedience,

eyes narrowing with too early wit, the old-fashioned
white linen collar wider than his shoulders.

A child, not the man who would stand
in the light of the kitchen, naked,
looking me straight in my own child's eyes.

What have I done
What have I done

Why have I entered this place as a girl,
left a thing unnamed? Why didn't I stay
in my room, pray for the best that night?

I was too greedy, that's it.
The kitchen called me.

Bread, jelly, lots of milk is what I wanted,
not to see my father naked in the light.
I'm closing my eyes to that memory.

I can still see him
I can still see him

Now.
I'll open my eyes and see the little boy instead—
face like my own,

what a glory of a smile!
This child will let me sleep through my life.

He won't climb in my bed,
leaving the scrim of bad dreams.
This little boy.

I love him
I love him

I like to think of my father this way
before he is changed into what I should not say.
He rides on a train headed west into the unknown,

away from his only home, away from his milk
breath clouding the prairie morning.

Suddenly in Grace

How in the bowl the collards steamed,
hiding gifts of meat and tomatoes.
How the chicken was cloaked
in its brown robe of singing fat.
How the cornbread could have been supper alone,
had been to others in starved times.

Again, look at the table.
How my mother plucked the greens
from her modest garden out back
and through the summer she chased
away creatures from the tomatoes,
righteously planting marigolds.
How she could have grown corn
so tall, she said, if only she had the land.
How her hands did not wring this chicken's
neck but her mother's did another.

Again.
How she baptized the greens in gallons
of water, scrubbed the stiff, unforgiving leaves.
How her back was turned to me
where she stood at the sink.
How she kept from speaking to my anger, lips tucked,
a bland face, head bowed suddenly in grace.
How she was determined to feed me.

Again.
How she plunged the greens over and over,
watched the water run free of dirt
and tried to teach me this way back,
though I had no interest then.
How she finally taught me, insistent.
How a last meal must be clean.

The Subject of Gardening

With sharecropper sorrow,
my mother looks at the empty field,
tells you a hard story, *I don't care*
what they're trying to grow here now.
All that there used to be cotton
and it won't give them nothing else.
Once, I labored in the garden with this woman,
her hands gritty, line of soil under her nails.
I was a careless girl loving the edible
smell of turned dirt. And who was that child
holding the grasshopper cupped in a palm?
Who made fun of beetles' frantic scrabbling?

These days I won't listen to the bent-backed
message in my mother's voice.
She'll tell me she found the road's end
but don't ask how she stumbled there.
I find it hard to go outside in the heat,
to keep the jade alive in its indoor pot,
to heap apologies on the browning edges,
to lay me down beside the truth of this land.

Days Are Plain

Rage has its moments and sympathies,
but some days are plain, if not uncomplicated.

The bird outside makes a fuss.
I call out, *Hey*—my Langston exhortation—

and that bird has the nerve to plant his feet
in my grass and keep on singing.

Or, my neighbor boy knocks bright and soon
on my apartment door. He's thirty years

younger than I, but this child
knows love is graceful.

I hand him a dollar for his missing tooth,
give an excuse as I close the door,

Sugar, I'm in the middle of writing a poem.
I don't want him to see I'm crying—

he's taught me one thing I needed
after so much time, this long time.

Or, I miss the hot arms of the South,
the old men who sell fresh produce

from their roadside stands.
I'm feeling the hunger for the fruit of my youth

when I drive to the grocery store
for the bag of peaches, bite into one, and yes,

the juice is scant, but who cares? Some days,
I walk through my small rooms with stingy

bits of home on my tongue and I give praise.
You know I just give praise.

Eatonton (One)

The eyes of marked cows reproach me.
Is this motherland where I am driven
under the canopy of trees?

This town, where our family
of women try to escape him?
You'll be back, he says,

but I live with Mama and my sisters
in the rented house,
walk barefoot, ignore threats of lockjaw,

dare to integrate the county pool,
though soon I have it to myself.
Cross the railroad tracks from blackening

edges, pass the county jail where striped
men never fail to call out their innocence
again and again.

I let my grammar and my accent slide,
learn the ways of folk:
a hard head makes for a soft behind.

So don't answer the phone ever,
and *come here, girl* to my mother's side,
and don't believe a man's words,

especially when he makes me a bargain.
I want to remain in this rusty earth place,
in the yard with snakes licking

in a blackberry patch. For now,
nothing scares me one bit.
There's cobbler every evening after supper.

I hold onto the funk
of neckbones and greens.

Reunion Scripture

I am all of them, they are all of me, I am me, they are thee . . .
—ETHERIDGE KNIGHT

1.

I am full in seconds on my first day in this backyard of kin—from
the heat punched to the face, the smell of fried fish on a meatless Friday.
Already, I am strange. I've started watching people close, bluffed by the
children running, disappearing around corners. Where have they gone?
Are they coming back?

My mother lays a hand on my arm. *No, he's not here.* She means the
great uncle, my dead grandmother's brother, a man who'll be arrested
soon, a man notorious in the family though no one calls his name if they
can help it. The one who never molested me (I don't think) though he
did my friend who lives across the street and some other folk walking
around here.

Go fix yourself a plate. My mother's eyes wide when she informs me
the old man's much too feeble to do anymore harm. *Forget about it.* As if
the strange gift this great-uncle carries from blood to itching fingertips
can't appear in one of my mother's brothers or sisters, in a cousin, in
me. As if he couldn't show up and be welcomed. Invited to sit down in
this yard of the dead, given comfort and a plate of light bread and hot
fish: a Jesus miracle.

2.

Service is out at Flat Rock Primitive Baptist, the first house of God
I ever knew, when my mama drove me down here each June so I
wouldn't turn into a heathen.

I've come back here for someone to embrace me. I want to feel
the swaying from years ago when my grandmother took me and my
friend, a neighbor girl, to worship here with my family. I want to hear
somebody pray at the huge rock the church is named for and where

I hope the spirits ride. I'm going to belt out my loudest voice. I just know I'm Mahalia reborn when I remember the rock is gone, dug up a while back and busted into gravel.

My friend still lives in that old house across the way, and says she loved my grandma, now dead, who used to bathe and dress her and comb her hair before Sunday services. And never failed to feed her plenty after. My friend doesn't blame my grandmother for the great-uncle who caught her wrong in the back bedroom sometimes after church. She isn't mad at my grandmother, either, for sitting right in the living room, singing spirituals to cover up the noise. She sang *One Morning Soon* or *Wade in the Water*. On a good day, *I Know I've Been Changed*.

Why I Will Praise an Old Black Man

Who lays in the cut, leaning back
in the dusty front seat of a long car he bought
on ancient credit, Al Green or a song
even deeper playing on the eight-track,
song about a working brother's calloused
pain, dismissed but throbbing the same.
This is the countrified, steady paycheck
man who braved sorrow song days, toiled
until his bones protested at last.
Who will die clean and grieved
like Charlie and Ambrose
and Vess and Lil Jinx.
I look to meet them in the yonder,
souls whose rheumy squints
have glimpsed tall trees over my head.

I have known some ugliness
but never at these hands that know how to whittle
from the wood's heart, that can gentle
a bad dog's growl with a slight wave.
That's why I got me a weakness
for the sharp-as-a-mosquito's-peter
creases in pinstriped pants, the Stacy Adams'
side-zipped shoe blues dance
of a dapper, old black man.
Yes, his musty do-right smell of cedar,
yes, his deacon's bass resting
in his throat on fourth Sunday morning,
yes, the way he calls me *daughter*
and then I can sleep
unbroken through the night.

What Grief Is

after Phillip Levine

We stand in line outside the church
in a hierarchy of grief. You know what grief is.
If you are reading a poem, this poem,
and never read another, you are sensitive
enough to know what grief is. Ok, back to me.
It isn't easy labor to figure out who gets
to be where in a solemn procession.
Some of the mourners get pushy,
and they have to be reminded.
His wife and his children and each grandchild go first.
Then his brothers and sisters, six of them,
and his nieces and nephews.
We fill up the pews on the right-hand side
(that place of God) and the amen corner as well.
The left side is for the sinners and for the friends,
the minor relatives, the professional funeral attendees,
and his brothers from the Lodge.
We sing his favorite spiritual,
One Morning Soon, the handkerchiefs
flutter the air like new breath
and there's an old-time preacher sounding off trying
to get somebody to shout but Mama is proud
Flat Rock Primitive Baptist is a dignified place today.
This would be easier for me long distance
instead of up close to the front
where my mother's brother lies, looking natural,
the hood open on his casket like his pickup truck.
God, he did love that truck.
Just about every country man does.
I wish I were back at the reception hall
with the volunteer sisters, frying up chicken

and pork chops, stirring macaroni and cheese,
maybe baking a pound cake,
not next to my mother who is weeping
(only the fifth time I can recall) for the one
who killed her cat by accident and was too
damned pretty and wild in his youth.
I pat her back and try to play grown.
That is the work of women, to pretend for others,
so I give a weak hug despite my surprise
that dying is such a brisk business.
This is the weight of what grief is.
Here is where I am supposed to end,
but no, I see my mother's brother,
basso profundo,
as he stands next to the barbecue grill,
the one made from blackened iron tubs,
and he holds a can of the Budweiser he drank
before he found the Lord and got saved
and the hundreds of stories he tells go
on and come back around again
and I hear the sizzling of good pigmeat,
the sustenance it will bring
once it is done cooking,
but for now, it sings a hymn that rises
from beneath Alvester's fingers.

Hawk Hoof Tea

My mother lost an eye to a butcher
knife when she was only five or six.
I've told this story before,
but as I age, her life becomes
a lesson,
how, if a family had not been poor and black,
a woman would be able to see
on both sides of her face.

As a daughter, I feel my mother's
phantom grief, but she reports the whole
thing very matter of fact, and ends
the tale
with pride: she was the best student when
she re-entered school after two absent years.
The best student and only one eye.

You have to hear that tale first before
you can realize the day the measles crept
into a house of children, that crowded space.
The presence of Sickness,
antagonist,
and again, the threat of absence.
Mama could have lost her remaining sight
because she lived in Georgia woods
and no doctor or money and her skin was not white
and her mother and father were hapless.

Then, there arrived Great-Grandpa Henry,
the son
of a full-blood Cherokee woman
whose own story got lost, but what
we do know is Henry walked in the door
and cured my mama and her brothers and sisters.

This is a spiritual awakening, sure enough.
Who wouldn't want to claim a medicine
woman and her son as blood, make him
a king
behind a small act? That's what writers do,
but did Henry seem copper royalty,
especially deep and profound?

No, Mama says. Henry was a cranky old man,
long-lived, over a hundred years—
he frowned whatever the season.
And his saving her and the others, his causing
a miracle?
Well, Henry did what he had to do, out
of love or impatience with dying.
He boiled down a hawk hoof into a tea,
but who knew if that was really the cure,
or even what a hawk hoof might be?

A bird's talon, a flower, a root?
Whatever it was, Mama drank a teacup full—
it tasted nasty, too.

Oklahoma Naming

I cried when I moved out here
and saw trees so short and few,
the prairie altogether flat,
and earth near scarlet like my Georgia

earth but that's where kinship ended.
And then, the land started hurting me
like an amputated part of my body.
And then, I had the dreams again

where my dead father appeared
with unusual cruelties.
I could not believe anything—
that's what visions taught me,

but when I became grateful
for deception, a new insistence,
my long-gone Indian grandmother
who came to me and I could speak

her words and I knew they were true.
When she left me, though, I laughed
at my foolishness. I have relatives
out here—though I can't prove it—

cousins many times removed
with last names telling something useful.
How many enemies our ancestors killed.
What kind of song a wounded animal makes.

Sometimes I wonder what would
be my name if I had to choose again.
My father's daughter might be called,
Woman-Who-Still-Loves-And-Cannot-Say-Why.

My grandmother's child,
Woman-Who-Pretends-Her-Visions-Are-Lies.

Upon Learning That My Indian Student Is a Sundancer

chant   good pain   pegs
medicine   chant   hits   fear
screechbird   chant   song
root   chant   fruit   billie's
tree   chant

you tell   piercing   days
days   days   days
i want   i want   grandmother
cherokee   story   she stayed
lost   georgia   here   hiding
black man   husband   child

or

blues trail   oklahoma   she walked
black man   husband   child
newborn   here   behind
blood   grandmother   there
screams   frontier

yes   lowdown   yes   sun
pegs   ripping   sound   guns
prayer   sigh   chant   prayer
tobacco   prayer   chant

i know   too late
grandmother   i don't
her name   her name   her name
grandmother   say   prairie

or

red clay   she knew   fever
hawk hoof   children   say
chant   tea   love   holy
mother   blind eye   kiss
dark   way   mark   she knew

Notes

"Red Clay Suite" is for A. Van Jordan.

"Passing" is for Terry Bozeman. The epigraph by Circe Sturm is from Sturm's book *Blood Politics: Race, Culture, and Identity in the Cherokee Nation of Oklahoma* (University of California Press, 2002). The phrase *atsi nahsa'i* means "ones who are owned." The definition is included in *Blood Politics* but originally printed in a quote by Theda Purdue in her book *Slavery and the Evolution of Cherokee Society, 1540–1866* (University of Tennessee Press, 1979). The Cherokee Freedmen are descendants of black slaves and Cherokees. They consider themselves full members of the tribe but were denied the right to vote in the tribal elections. On June 18, 1984, several Freedmen filed a class action suit with the Department of Justice. According to *Blood Politics*, they claimed that they "had been denied the right to vote and tribal benefits from federal funds because their lack of verifiable Cherokee blood prevented them from obtaining registration cards."

"Giving Thanks for Water" is for Remica L. Bingham. According to the Tulsa Historical Society, on the morning of May 30, 1921, Sarah Page, a white elevator operator, accused Dick Rowland of grabbing her arm. Newspapers eventually reported that Rowland was accused of raping Page, though the crime was unsubstantiated. On June 1, 1921, white rioters descended on Black Tulsa. Twenty-four hours later, the thirty-five city blocks that made up the African American community of Tulsa had been burned to the ground. Early reports estimated that thirty-six people, both black and white, had died; later, however, the Tulsa Race Riot Commission estimated the number of African Americans killed to be well over three hundred.

"An Angel, Unaware": The line "Mrs. Williams' face was pleading when she spoke of her god to me" is quoted from "When She Spoke of God" by Lance Jeffers, *My Blackness Is the Beauty of this Land* (Broadside Press, 1970).

"Blues Aubade (or, Revision of the Lean, Post-Modernist Pastorale)" is for J. W. Richardson Jr.

"Mister Buzzard and Brother Crow": The line "Nigger, your breed ain't metaphysical" is quoted from "Pondy Woods" by Robert Penn Warren, *The Collected Poems of Robert Penn Warren* (Louisiana State University Press, 1998). The line "Cracker, your breed ain't exegetical" is quoted from an unpublished interview of Sterling A. Brown conducted by Steven Jones (May 4 and 14, 1978; on file at the Institute for Arts and Humanities and the Afro-American Resource Center, Howard University).

"dirty south moon" is for Riché Richardson. According to Phillip Dray, *At the Hands of Persons Unknown: The Lynching of Black America* (Modern Library, 2003), Mary Turner of Brooks County, Georgia, was eight months pregnant when she was lynched by a white mob sometime between the 17th and the 24th of May in 1918; her husband, Haynes, had been lynched by the same mob days earlier, and when Mary threatened to call the law, the mob turned on her. The bodies of both Mary and her unborn child were mutilated. The lines "she is / rounder than the moon / and far more faithful" are quoted from "song at midnight" by Lucille Clifton, *The Book of Light* (Copper Canyon, 1993).

"Poem for Birds": The line "I know why the caged bird sings" is from "Sympathy" by Paul Lawrence Dunbar, *The Complete Poems of Paul Lawrence Dunbar* (Dodd Mead, 1993).

"Another Easter Poem" is for Jimmy.

"Their Splendid": The lines "I love your laughter arrogant and bold / You are too splendid for this city street" are from "Sonnet to a Negro in Harlem" by Helene Johnson, printed in *This Waiting for Love: Helene Johnson, Poet of the Harlem Renaissance*, edited by Verner D. Mitchell (University of Massachusetts Press, 2000)

"Days Are Plain" is for Saxon Calhoun.

"Eatonton (One)" is for Natasha Trethewey.

"Reunion Scripture": The line "I am all of them, they are all of me, I am me, they are thee" is from "The Idea of Ancestry" by Etheridge Knight, printed in *The Essential Etheridge Knight* (University of Pittsburgh Press/ Pitt Poetry Series, 1986).

"Why I Will Praise an Old Black Man" is for Herman Beavers.

"What Grief Is" is for Alvester James.

"Upon Learning That My Indian Student Is a Sundancer" is for Faron Bear and Gabrielle Jesiolowski.